Dedication

To Mumsy & Daddio:
Thank you for having me.

Understand Me:
My Story About Psychosis, Recovery, and God's Grace

A reminder from Me:

"Fear is temporary, regret is forever".

- Rochelle L V Devonish

Preface

Hey, Chelle here.

This is a story about a part of my life.

Mental ill health is a difficult subject. For me, it brought with it feelings of guilt and shame.

I did not know how to explain what had happened to me, and to be honest, I did not want to. I was lost, confused, and had no idea who I was.

This is an account of events that occurred before, during, and after mental ill health; written as best as I can remember them. The moments recorded here may be painful to read and could be distressing…but they are part of my journey.

I must note here though, that I was not and am not by myself on this journey called life. My story would not be complete or even exist without God.

It is God's grace that has kept me alive...I have not done anything to deserve it, and I am not better than you, reading this right now. It is God that came and found me. It was God who saved me, and God carries me still.

The footprints in the sand are not my own.

So, I wrote this book as a testimony of what God has done and continues to do in my life.

I would also like for mental health to be a part of every conversation, and for the words I have written to help someone else, even if that is one person.

When you are standing in front of a mirror, you look at your reflection. However, there is a distinct difference between looking at yourself and seeing who you really are.

I hope that, through this narrative, you will know that it is okay not to be okay. That things can, and do, get better…and that you should never give up.

My story is not a pleasant one and it is not easy to tell - but it is important.

It is important because recovery is possible.

Even when you feel lonely, I want you to know that you are not alone.

God is with you and will never leave you.
All you need to do, is trust him.

God's got you.
Let's go.

CHAPTERS

I. Stress

"Rochelle...Rochelle..."

"Rochelle...do you know where you are?"

I gave the name of the Hospital.

"That's right".

I had no idea who she was.

I was answering, but I had no idea who I was either.

All I was wondering to myself was – how did I get here?

2011

I can remember waking up and having a shower. I also remember being told that I should stay at home and take the day off work. But I didn't (and wouldn't) listen. I was determined to be there for others, and I didn't want to let anyone down.

That…was one of a series of mistakes that I made that day.

I put my work clothes on and picked up my Bible. I did not normally carry my Bible with me to work, but just felt like I would need it that day. I am not sure why…but I felt strongly about it.

I also had another book with me – Blackstone's Criminal Practice; this is a legal text that may be used by practitioners. Even though I was working in a Law Office at the time, I did not normally have this with me either.

I put my shoes on and left the house, without a cardigan or coat, in late November.

Somehow, (although I don't know how), I was then on a public road. Everyone and everything around me was moving at an increased pace, but I wasn't really paying attention to that – I just wanted to make it to work.

The next thing I knew, I was at a bus stop. This would later become what I now call a '**Grace moment**'.

A **'Grace moment'** is when God saves you from something, but you don't know it at the time.

It includes being removed from a situation, being diverted from making a bad decision, or being redirected when you're going the wrong way.

Sometimes, it can even mean being saved from yourself.

I needed to get the bus so that I could get to the train station. However, I didn't have any money with me. I also had no bank cards and had left my travel card at home. I don't think I had my mobile phone either, although this would not have helped, as it was not yet possible to pay from a phone.

All this together, meant that I was unable to pay my bus fare. The bus driver was also not prepared to let me travel without paying and, in the end, drove off without me.

This was at least five **Grace moments** rolled into one.

The next thing I remember, is that there was a woman in green talking to me. I would later realise that she was a Paramedic, but I did not recognise this at the time.

The other thing to note here, is that, between the location where the bus stop was and where the Paramedic spoke to me, there are at least 7 crossings that I made across public roads.

Somehow, I had made it across all these roads without getting hurt or inadvertently causing a collision that may have hurt someone else. There are so many **Grace moments** here that I am unable to count them. However, what I do know, is that it was God that kept me safe.

The Paramedic seemed to be telling me that I needed to go with her...but I just wanted to keep going. I felt very confused and disorientated, with no understanding as to why the Paramedic was trying to stop me. I attempted to explain that I was trying to get to work, but it felt like no one was listening to what I had to say.

The Police then arrived...which only served to make me even more agitated. I felt like I needed to escape – so I ran away again and again. However, I did not get very far.

As far as I can remember, I was eventually detained on the tarmac/pavement/road. I think that I was placed into handcuffs, although I am unable to confirm this given how unwell I was. I can vaguely recall being brought to my feet.

Then...everything went black.

II. Isolation

"Rochelle…Rochelle…"

"Rochelle…do you know where you are?"

I gave the name of the hospital.

"That's right".

It was the Paramedic again. She was walking me through the Hospital, turning down corridors I did not completely recognise, ending up at a small room. The Police were still there - they would subsequently assist the Paramedic with getting me into the room.

I am not sure how long I was in there for.

I was experiencing auditory hallucinations, and delusions of grandeur. It is difficult to know whether I had visual hallucinations as well; everything felt real to me, so I may never actually know. This was the most frightening part –

the not knowing: who I was, where I was, why I was there or what would happen to me.

I can recall being in conversation with and sitting across from a Nurse. He was asking me for my jewellery. I attempted as much as I could to explain that I was not going to hurt myself with it (or anything else). Unfortunately, that narrative was not believed.

After some time, I was moved to another room – it was a white room with a different Nurse outside. It had a small window in the door (presumably so that the Nurse could watch and check on me), but there were no other windows or doors through which you could enter or exit. I genuinely believed that this would be my life...that I was not going to get out of Hospital, and that my future, would be limited to that small white room.

I should perhaps explain here that, the Hospital gave out medication in small white cups. Tablets were counted and placed inside of the cup, which would be waiting at the medication station. All I had to do was swallow them, open my mouth to show that they were gone, and return the cup empty.

I was very scared about this whole process – how could I make sure that my tablets weren't confused with somebody else's? Even if they were for me, how would I know whether they were at the right dose? What if I had a negative reaction to them, and long would I be taking them for? Why was I taking them in any event? I was confused, afraid and felt alone.

But at that point, there was another **Grace moment** – the one that I think about the most.

I am not sure where the Nurse was, but I don't remember her being outside the room at this point. All I knew was, I felt the urge to sing. I stood up and started singing the first verse of 'Amazing Grace' as loud as I could. I just sang it over and over again, whilst looking out of the window in the door.

I could see a man outside of the room...or at least, a figure resembling a man. He was some distance from the room, yet he was looking directly at me. He had a friendly face and was sort of smiling. An angel sent by God.

He made a gesture that I hope I never forget – his right hand was shaped as if he was holding one of the white medicine cups. Then, he raised his hand to his lips, as if he was taking some medication. After that, he pointed upwards (towards the sky) with his index finger. At that point, I knew...I knew that it was a message from God – to take my medication so that I could get better...to keep singing and never stop. It was God, and his Grace.

It was then that I realised that I was going to be okay. **Grace moment.**

III. Grace

Eventually, I was moved from the white room onto a ward. The best thing about this was:

   1) I had my own room with a door that I could close;

   2) there were board games available for me to play.

I have always loved board games – well, any game to be honest. But board games have a special place in my heart. Whether it's Chess, Scrabble, Backgammon or Monopoly…I look forward to creating new memories with the ones I love.

Whilst in hospital, I was able to spend time with family playing Chess and Scrabble. This is one of my favourite memories of being on that ward. I couldn't play for long periods, because my medication made me extremely tired and sluggish. However, that did not stop me from being on course for a win.

My other favourite ward moment...was being pampered and getting my nails done.

I used to bite my nails when I was younger, but I had started growing and painting them not long before my admission to hospital.

I will be the first to admit that I am OPI obsessed. OPI is a brand of nail lacquer, and each shade has a different name. I have the special skill of being able to recall the names of most (if not all) of my OPI collection, just by description or looking at the colour. When my nails were painted, it was with one of my top-ten colours at that time – Bogota Blackberry. I love Bogota Blackberry...a rich deep red cherry with a hint of mischievousness. This is one of the colours that reflects me (the mischievousness in particular). It was exactly what I needed, and in that, came an important lesson...that I had to take care of myself.

It was at that point that I started to realise that it was okay to put myself first. This is so hard because I had spent so much time believing that, in putting myself first, I was being selfish - but that was not it at all. In fact, the opposite was true; I had consistently put myself last – caring for myself very little and exhausting myself in trying to do so much for everyone else that my cup was empty. I wasn't pouring into myself at all. That's what got me so ill - I had forgotten about what was important; me.

Grace moment.

Those close to me came to visit me a lot whilst I was in hospital. I don't think that they really know how much this meant to me.

On one occasion, they came with a close friend. This was another angel. As we sat together, the angel sang me part of song – "Never Would Have Made it" by Marvin Sapp.

I remember the moment with my angel vividly. It is one of the few things that I can recall from my time in hospital, and I sincerely hope that this memory remains with me for the rest of my life. It humbled me and reintroduced gratitude and appreciation into my life.

"Never Would Have Made it" is another one of those songs that I know God sent to me. This song is all about giving glory to God for all that he has done. It is a message to me that I would not be where I am without God, that he will never leave me and that I cannot do anything without him. I am only here because of God's grace, and I am still alive because God saved me. **Grace moment.**

Whilst I was in hospital, the radio was on Magic FM, and as far as I can remember, it played most of the time.

One of the more distressing parts of my experience and my illness, were the hallucinations and the delusions of grandeur – I thought that the songs played on the radio were about me, and if there were lyrics, those were a message to me too. I didn't realise the impact that this was having on me at the time. I interpreted everything negatively and took everything personally. Until I heard Take That.

It was their song 'Rule the World' that did it. It was played on repeat whilst I was on the ward, and I loved it. It encouraged a change in me and fuelled my belief that I was going to be okay. It made me feel like recovery was possible, like I shouldn't give up, and that I had a light inside of me that the world needed to experience. I love 'Rule the World' most when it plays unexpectedly on my phone or on the radio...the first two words with those first two notes, ("You light..."), always bring me back to myself.

It will forever be one that changed my life.

I can remember walking with a nurse to the medication room. The medication room was a room with what I call a 'stable door' – the kind of door where the top can be open whilst the bottom stays closed. I used to join the queue outside this room and wait for my turn when my medication would be handed to me in that familiar white cup. Medication had to be taken at the stable door, with the hospital staff checking that all tablets had been swallowed before being allowed to walk away.

This visit to the medication room was different however... this time, I was taken inside. The Nurse retrieved two books that I believe were on the shelf – one was orange and the other was green. Both were quite large. The Nurse proceeded to open the green one and was turning the pages as if she was looking for something. Once she had found what she was searching for, she put the book in front of me with the pages open at a particular section. As far as I can remember, it was the section starting with 'P'.

The Nurse used her index finger to point at a word in the book.

Nurse: "Can you read that?"

Me: "Yes"

Nurse: "What does it say…?"

Me: … "Psychosis"

I did not understand what it meant, nor did I know why it meant that I was in hospital; but that was the first time I had a word that could be used to describe my illness.

Nurse: "this is what happened to you."

Whilst in hospital, the medical and support staff would arrange supervised activities – I presume to allow those on the ward to have positive experiences in a safe environment.

I think I went to the gym a couple of times. I didn't know it then, but the gym would become extremely important to me, and indispensable in improving my mental health.

In general, the staff at the hospital were kind to me, encouraging me to try new activities and making sure that I was safe. I don't know whether I will get the opportunity to thank each of them in person the way that I would like, but the gratitude and appreciation is there all the same.

I'm not sure how long I was in hospital before I was allowed to go outside of the ward. However, I vaguely remember going outside of the hospital at some point. I don't know exactly where I went to, but I was glad to be outside. By this time, Christmas was approaching, but the sun was still shining.

There is something special about the warmth of the sun in winter. I've since learnt from a new friend that there is a word for this; 'apricity'.

I loved the feeling of the sun on my skin. It was beautiful.

It felt like renewal. **Grace moment.**

It felt like I was free.

IV. Fear

I was in hospital for almost a month before I was discharged and allowed to go home.

I still had a team to help me - I vaguely remember that they would talk to me, but to be honest, I am unable to recall the content of some of those conversations. It was so strange...I was trying to learn how to do things from scratch, making sure that I took my medication so that I would get better. It was like somebody had hit a 'reset' button on my life. In essence, I had to get to know myself all over again.

It was not just about the clothes I would wear or the books I would read. It was more than that. I had to rediscover the things that were important to me – those things that were part of my character before I became unwell. This was one of the most difficult parts of my journey; I was trying to be who I was before my illness, but at the same time, I did not want to be that version of myself out of fear that I would relapse. I was anxious and scared, but I found it difficult to articulate these emotions to other people.

I did not want those around me to interpret my fear as an indication that I would have another episode, so I started to withdraw. However, on the inside, I was feeling so many different things:

- **Sadness**. I was going to have to let go of who I had been. The me that had been pretending to be okay.

- **Anger**. I had not taken care of myself at all. I had been focusing on making sure everyone else was okay and had forgotten about myself.

- **Lonely**. It was like a vicious circle – I isolated myself and didn't speak to anyone about how I truly felt. There was no way for others to know what I was really going through, but I didn't want to explain this to them either. This meant I was still trying to do everything alone, and the fact that I was alone in turn fed the loneliness.

- **Lost.** I did not know who I was or what would happen to me moving forward. I felt defined by my illness – like no one would or could love and accept me because of it.

- **Confused.** I did not understand why God had chosen me to experience Psychosis.

- **Disappointed**. I felt like a I had failed at meeting the expectations I had for myself.

- **Anxious.** It just felt like something bad was going to happen, all the time.

- **Afraid.** I did not know what would happen next or whether I was ready for it.

After my episode of Psychosis, I was more afraid that I had ever been before.

Afraid of life.

Afraid of myself.

No one can prepare you for an experience that is not 'real'. It is like having a meaningful conversation with a loved one...the type of conversation you really appreciate and are grateful for...then, the next day, your loved one explains to you that the conversation did not happen.

You may be insistent and incredulous about this, (the idea that the conversation was not real), after all, you can remember talking to them as well as their responses. You can say where the conversation took place, what you were wearing at the time and even what was said. But in truth... it really did not happen.

This is what psychosis was like for me – experiencing thoughts and physical sensations that others didn't. Those around me did not see what I was seeing, smell what I was smelling, or hear the things I was hearing. I lost touch with life and all semblance of reality - like a large wave that is overwhelming and powerful; no matter how well you can swim, you feel like you're drowning. I felt scared about what Psychosis would mean for my future – for relationships, work, and family. I had so many questions, but a lot of them remained in my head and so, were unanswered. Would I be able to travel? What about insurance? And driving a vehicle? Could I still donate blood? And how do I accept that it my episode is a part of me now?

I felt frustrated and upset about what had happened to me. I was also angry. Blaming myself for my illness and being extremely self-critical. I wasn't 'present' at all. Not really. I became a perfectionist – I did not take risks anymore and, to be honest, I wasn't living life. I was just existing.

I would look in the mirror, but I did not recognise the person looking back at me. It's a weird feeling...not knowing who you are. But that is what happened to me.

I just did not know where to turn. I felt like no one could help me and that I was too 'broken' to be saved.

Then, I did what my angel told me and looked up –

I turned to God.

V. Surrender

I can't quite remember exactly how it happened, but at some point, I learnt about a choir. I really wanted to go, but was apprehensive, holding back and had lost my confidence. I prayed, talked to God, and tried to find the courage within me to join. However, I was still relying on myself to get to the choir rehearsal, and still leaning on what I thought I knew.

It seems to be part of the human condition to want to be in control. To think that we decide what happens next. To believe that our plans are the ones that succeed. I held these beliefs and ways of thinking for a long time, wanting to make the rules, build my own foundation, and carve my own path.

I had always been an independent soul, intent on following my plans and extremely obstinate. I wanted my life to go a certain way, and Psychosis had not been part of that.

I had not foreseen that I would become so unwell (or become unwell at all) and did not think there would ever be a time when I would not recognise myself. Moreover, I did not want to admit that I had experienced an episode of Psychosis - mostly because I was averse to being labelled as 'crazy' – but also because it meant that I had lost control.

Notwithstanding, trying to do everything myself (and doing things my way) was not successful to any extent or at all. As far as I can remember, I was yet to contact the choir about joining and was feeling apprehensive about singing in public. With my confidence low and self-belief non-existent, it would soon become clear to me that I had to do something else that was new to me.

I had to surrender.

> *Surrender* is fully submitting to God's plans and that the implementation of those plans is to be done <u>God's way</u>.

I had no other option but to humble myself, accept help and admit that I had been wrong all along. There was only one way to turn: towards God. I had to trust him – wholly, completely and with everything I had.

This was an important lesson for me. Albeit I did not learn it the first time. To be honest, I am still learning it now.

When I initially tried it, I surrendered through words alone. I said that I was surrendering and thought that was enough. My focus was on what I wanted, and when I wanted it. However, I quickly learnt that this is not the way God works – conversely, everything will happen on his time and his time alone. Surrendering was not about me at all…and my 'plan' was immaterial. **Grace moment.**

The next time I surrendered, I did it physically. I knelt with my hands out and closed my eyes. The problem with this was – I wanted to be seen. I thought that if God saw me in such a pose, he would give me what I wanted when and how I wanted it. However, I was very much mistaken.

I would keep making mistakes for some time…mostly because I thought that the process of surrender was about my wants, desires, and needs. I was impatient and unwilling to compromise. On top of that, I am determined and stubborn - a bad combination. I wanted to go to the choir, and I wanted to sing. It seemed simple to me at the time – so why wasn't I able to do it?

I had to learn a very important truth - that God comes first. Furthermore, that God loves all his children; I was not going to be prioritised before anyone else, nor was I preferred over anyone else.

I once read that "sometimes, you don't get what you want. Not because you don't deserve it, but because you deserve so much more." My focus had been on turning up to the choir and singing a song. I was not particularly concerned about the genre or style. I did not really have an idea about what was best for my voice or what part I should sing – anything would do. Nonetheless, what I would start to learn, was that God wanted more from my life…and a lot more from me. This was difficult for me, because I did not think I had anything 'special' to give, especially not after my episode of Psychosis.

But (**Grace moment**), I was wrong.

I will not lead you to believe that surrender is easy at all. It isn't. It is different for everybody. For me, it includes the changing of actions, thoughts, words, and attitudes that have existed so that I can fulfil God's purpose for my life. It means accepting that I am not in control and do not know myself at all.

Surrendering is also a commitment. It is not a singular practice that is carried out once and forgotten about. Conversely, it is repeated, again and again, and is a necessary process throughout life. In my journey, I tried to keep an open mind and an open heart to the possibility that surrender could work, but I had to humble myself. I had to accept that my life was not my own. Then, one day...I tried again. I made the decision to surrender every part of me - mental, physical, spiritual, and emotional. I had to surrender it all and give my soul to God and his purpose for me.

Sometime later, I was on my way to the choir.

The songs we sang were designed to improve mental health and increase confidence. I practiced singing techniques, explored different genres of music, and learnt songs that I had not known before. I was in my element, and as far as I can remember, I stayed with the choir for the whole term.

When I sang, I did not think about Psychosis. I did not think about the stresses of life or what was going to happen next. I did not think at all, which was new for me, and I loved it.

The choir taught me an invaluable lesson: I did not get everything I wanted, but God blessed me with what I had needed. All I had to do, was get out of my own way.

Grace moment.

It was more than just singing – it was medicine for my soul.

VI. Recovery

I had many different teams supporting me after my episode of Psychosis. Psychiatrists made sure that my medication was at an accurate level, and I had nurses and a support team that helped me to identify how I'd become so ill in the first place. There were psychologists, providing coping strategies and the tools I would need to try and address my anxiety. It was indispensable to have a space that I could go to – somewhere non-judgemental, unbiased, and safe.

I had approximately 5 years of treatment, medical sessions, and appointments with those teams before I would feel like I was getting close to what I'd hoped for.

Recovery.

It was then that God introduced a second choir into my life. I was so nervous. The 'what ifs' were taking over my brain and it felt like I couldn't stop myself from worrying.

The questions in my head were so overwhelming: what if I didn't know the songs? What if I am unable to remember my part? What if I'm unable to sing at all?

The amount of overthinking I did was so extreme...I was agonising about anything and everything...and almost didn't go.

Then I decided to pray about it.

I was talking to God more and more, and trying to take the time to hear what he needed me to do. I am unable to remember where I was or when it took place, but there came a time when I received a command telling me to be courageous.

Courage to me was an alien concept – it was something other people had, but I did not think it applied to me. I was convinced that I was not the right person for this message – it felt like someone else was supposed to receive it. However, God makes no mistakes.

I tried extremely hard to be perfect...to rediscover my confidence. I wanted to be brave so that the fear would go away, but that didn't work. I really wanted to erase all my fear entirely so that I could achieve all that God had planned for me. However, removing my fear was not possible either.

I started to feel despondent, distant, and removed. It felt like, no matter what I tried, I remained as I was – insecure and afraid. I could not escape from my fear, I could not run away from my fear, and I could not erase my fear either. I would make statements like 'I'm too scared' and 'I'm just afraid'. Fear became the excuse I would use for any situation or interaction. After all, it was easier to blame fear for my inaction than it was to accept the truth: I was in my own way.

The whole experience was incredibly frustrating and confronting. I thought that recovery meant that I was completely 'healed' but thinking that way is dangerous.

These thoughts focused on the idea that I was a problem… they encouraged the idea that there was something wrong with me, that I needed to be 'fixed'. They also reinforced the idea that I was not courageous.

That was not and is not true.

It was during this time that I began to learn the true meaning of the word courage.

Courage means doing something even though you are afraid.

It is not the absence of fear.

Courage is <u>pushing through</u> the fear.

I had decided to take some time to pray about my illness, and, as far as I could, accept that it had happened. This is a process that continues to this day, and it led me to a discovery and a truth that I was not expecting; God loves me.

It was hard for me to accept this on a personal level. It had been difficult before my episode of psychosis, but during and after it, the idea that I was loved felt so foreign that I found it almost impossible to believe. The world will try to convince you that you are 'broken', that you are worthless and that you have no purpose - especially if you have been unwell for any reason. However, the opposite is true: each one of us is worthy, and every one of us has a purpose.

This truth applies to me as much as it does to you. Yes, you - reading this right now. If it is true that you are worthy (which you are) and that your life has a purpose in line with God's plan (which it does), it follows that you are loved.

God loves you too. He loves <u>all</u> of us – unconditionally and in an unlimited way.

The realisation that I was, and am, loved by God, led me to want to obey what I had been told – to be courageous.

So, I decided to go along to the second choir. I was anxious and apprehensive about it...but I did not want to give in to my fear. I say this now as if it was simple, but it really was not easy at the time. I had breathing exercises on my phone to keep me calm, listened to music to help with my anxiety, and approached each challenge one step at a time. It was not easy, but it was worth it. This was not achieved alone. To say that would be misleading. It was God guiding me, protecting me, moulding me, and ultimately saving me from myself.

All I needed to do, was believe in God and trust him completely.

VII. Faith

My obsession with Japan had existed well before my episode in 2011. I was determined to learn as much as I could about Japan and wanted to learn Japanese.

My imagination was completely consumed with the grand idea that I would go to Japan. I wanted to see everything for myself - learn more about the culture, find out more about its people and try new, different, delicious food options.

However, upon my admission to Hospital, I had almost given up on the idea. I genuinely believed that the Hospital was going to be my life from that point on. I did not believe that I could or would make it out, and I was on the edge of giving up on my dream.

But, around 2015, I started to think about Japan again. I really wanted to go…and I mean, really wanted to go.

So, I prayed about it.

> *Prayer* is bringing everything before God – good, bad,
>
> or in between – he will listen.
>
> It's also important to hear what God is saying to you.

I love prayer. It's the time I spend in fellowship with God. It does not matter that I am not perfect, and it does not matter that I have been and am – a sinner. God created me, knows everything about me and who I am. He hears my prayers before I say them and understands my heart without me having to use words. God is an integral part of my life – my constant, my saviour, my redeemer.

So, I prayed. I surrendered. I trusted that God would take me there...that one day, I would see Japan for myself. I believed that completely.

2016

As I walked down the jet bridge to board the plane, I could feel the tears building in my eyes. I was trying to breathe deeply so that I would not have a panic attack. I was really scared.

Scared beyond belief.

I found my seat on the plane. Bag stored overhead, I sat down, and put my seat belt on.

I always make sure that I read the safety card, no matter how much I fly. Flying is a fear that I had for a long time...so I always make sure that I read the card in case of an emergency.

I didn't know anyone. I had decided to travel by myself because I wanted to do something just for me. It was honestly one of the first times in my life when I had put myself first (after God of course).

Next, is what I refer to as, the 'push back'. When the plane is pushed away from the terminal in reverse and the engines are tested. I always know that, after 'push back', I am committing to being in the sky for a certain time, and that I need to trust God to get me to my destination.

After that comes the inevitable. The taxi towards the runway. Seat belt signs on, cabin checked, overhead compartments closed, plane doors secured. The cabin crew have completed their demonstrations in line with the safety video and have taken their seats too.

Then, the part of flying that I hate the most...

Take-off.

Engines revving, plane gaining speed. The acceleration, force, and sound of it...the feeling of the lift off the ground...weightless for a moment, completely suspended and ascending into the sky.

"Ladies and gentlemen, we would like to welcome you aboard this flight today. Journey time is approximately 12 hours and 50 minutes, and we will be flying non-stop to Tokyo. We thank you for choosing us for this flight to Japan."

It felt like forever.

I couldn't sleep – I rarely sleep on planes even though I'm normally exhausted. The 'what ifs' tend to keep me awake until the plane makes a safe landing at my intended destination. I had also wanted to see Japan...yes, I'm afraid of flying, but I can't help but to watch the landing (and take-off) process. Somehow, I feel safer when I watch it happen.

I just can't describe the feeling. It had been years since the idea of travelling to Japan had entered my mind...now I was going to be there.

There were more plane sounds and procedures to go through...the awful 'click' of the wheels coming down, the airplane 'banking' so that the pilot can turn and line the plane up into the right position, and the slow descent out of the clouds.

I could see land. I could see Japan.

It was so close.

Slowly and gradually, we got closer and closer. I could feel the tears already...the landing was imminent.

Then, the moment that I really hope I never forget for the rest of my life: when the wheels touched down on the runway. Rear ones first...then the front ones. I broke down then. All the tears, the emotion, the anticipation, anxiety, stress, and worry. I was crying like a baby, but I had made it. **Grace moment.**

I had landed in Japan.

It was also then that it really 'hit me'. All I had to do, was trust God and believe that he would do what he had promised. And that was what I did.

Five years after my hospital admission, I was on the other side of the world about to begin my Japanese adventure.

Grace moment

There was no doubt in my mind: God's got me.

VIII. Growth

Looking back on it, I needed to go to Japan to 'unlock' something that had been hidden for a long time. Something that I had almost forgotten about...

Myself.

In 2019, I bought myself a dress. A red dress.

I had intended to take it on a special break away and wear it on that break. I was excited and determined to focus on me and what I needed - so my plans were not going to change. I spent a lot of my time waiting for things around me to be perfect. I was 'holding on' to the red dress until the perfect time, and for the perfect place so that I could wear it at the perfect moment.

Now, in life, perfection does not exist...it is not real. However, the idea of perfection fit nicely as an excuse for me to stay well within my comfort zone. I was actively choosing to stay in a place where I was existing…I was just not living.

This realisation led to self-reflection, examination, and discovery of who I am and of what was important to me. It is one thing to identify the faults that others have and the mistakes that they may make, but looking at yourself in the mirror and recognising your own is another thing entirely. But that is what I had to do. I had to start the process of accepting that I wanted to grow as a person and needed to do so. I had to be willing to start somewhere.

No other human could do it for me.

As part of that journey, I had to admit that it was not other people that were the source of my anger and pain. Ultimately, I was responsible for that. I was the one that had not yet 'let go' of my past. The truth was (and is), that there was only one person in my way. That was (and is), me.

It is exceptionally difficult to listen to what is going on inside of you, especially in silence and solitude. To be alone with what you see – no one else to validate you, no one else to appreciate you and no one else to love you. It all must come from yourself. It is important to spend time with yourself and say with sincerity: "I am sorry", "I forgive you", "I love you".

This is one of the hardest processes I have had to begin in my life…and it has no end. It continues today.

The thing was, I still wasn't really living – the red dress was hidden away, safely stored in a place where I would be able to get to it when I eventually decided that it was the 'right time'. The shoes to go with it were intentionally kept out of sight so that no dust could fall on them. The handbag was left in a place where it was accessible but only once I was 'ready' to wear the dress.

The red dress was 'ready', but I wasn't. I felt confused and frustrated. I thought I had looked at my faults, examined my errors and 'changed my ways', so why hadn't that worked?

Well...the issue was in what I thought. I thought I had made a big step in just buying the dress, but in fact, my mindset was still the same. I was still waiting for 'the next day', 'the next time', the 'next moment' to start living. I was still hiding from the world.

I had a hoodie that I would wear with jeans. My hoodie had several functions...the most important function at the time being that I could stay in my comfort zone. It just made everything easier, or so I thought.

My logic then was – if I stay hidden, I could stay safe. No one would see my scars and wounds and take advantage of my vulnerabilities, no one would experience my pain and make fun of me for it, and no one would know how I really felt.

This meant that my hoodie went everywhere with me...and I mean <u>everywhere</u>. It was even with me on my trip to Japan - I told myself that it helped me feel less anxious on the plane...It didn't.

It wasn't until autumn of 2019 that I realised the truth about that hoodie. It was holding me back. It was keeping me in a place of fear and preventing me from growing as a person.

So, I took some time out and embarked on a journey of self-discovery. I won't say more than that here – that is a different story. However, what I started to learn was that I was in my own way. There was and is, no one and nothing between me and my destiny. I was the one that was allowing my fear to be in control.

There were so many discoveries I made during this period that helped me to grow out of the Rochelle that had been hidden. One of the realisations that I had was:

No one is going to know who you are, unless you tell them.

There were a lot of new things that I had always loved but hadn't dared to step out and try. Those things that I had locked away in childhood – that side of me that can do anything and knows it. Once I had discovered this, I had to come out of my shell – quite literally. It was liberating.

Towards the end of 2019, I wanted to try something different – I wanted to try something new. So, I decided that it was time for the red dress.

I put it on, (and yes, the shoes and the handbag were there too). I wore them all to a special event and honestly, I felt amazing. I felt beautiful...and for the first time in a long time, I felt like me.

For years, I had denied that I would ever become... 'a gym person'. As far as I was concerned, that was a place for people that were fit; people that were already in shape; people who were able to do aerobics and run on treadmills for 30 minutes without stopping. It was not for me.

I only started at the gym because it was identified as being positive for my mental health. I was keen to keep my recovery going after Psychosis, so I thought I would at least try.

I found myself a trainer.

My trainer during this period had, let's say, a unique approach to health, exercise, and wellbeing. It was not about going on a diet, cutting out food I loved or being on treadmills all the time. It was about what was right for me – mind, body, and soul.

At one stage, I was introduced to a 20kg sandbag. For some reason, my trainer had me push it across the floor of the gym from one end to the other, then I would get on a bike for at least 30 seconds and sprint it out.

I was using the 20kg sandbag for some time. However, my trainer then decided that I needed to get out of my comfort zone. It was at that stage that I was introduced to the sandbag that was 30kg.

My trainer asked if I could lift it. I just looked at them in disbelief. In my head I was thinking – but why? What sort of exercise is this? But there was no getting out of it. So, I lifted the 30kg sandbag and then threw it back onto the floor. I hope I never forget the look that my trainer gave me. It was a look that said, "I told you so".

I continued with the sandbags for a while, with changes to my workout regime over time...then, my trainer told me that they thought lifting weights would be the best thing for me.

I thought – 'no'. Firstly, I am a woman and did not want to be developing 'bodybuilder' type muscles (no offence to those that have them...I just was averse to having them myself). The other thing was, I did not see any other women in the weights section of the gym. I felt intimidated and I felt out of place.

Then I tried it.

I tried deadlifting...and I fell in love with it. At some point, I moved to another gym and found myself in my element...a gym where I could build myself up and lift more. A gym where I could be myself. I would soon discover the beauty that is my sledgehammer. In truth, it is not actually mine, but I act like it is.

All I need for a good stress busting session in the gym, is a sledgehammer, a tyre, and Janet Jackson's 'Rhythm Nation' playing in my ears. It's where I love to be. So, there I was...a gym person! The thing I had thought and said that I would never become. I was so wrong.

I fell in love with weights and wanted to do more lifting. I had told my trainer that I wanted to be able to deadlift

150kg...this plan was delayed and rearranged during the Covid-19 pandemic, until the gym re-opened. So, towards the end of 2020, I just went for it.

I deadlifted 150kg.

At that point, my trainer turns to me and says – "do you want to add a little bit more?" I wasn't expecting this, but they added another 10kg. I lifted it, and thus, I hit a deadlift of 160kg.

This was more than just a lift though. It was evidence of the fact that I could do more than what I thought I was capable of. In addition, it served as a reminder to me to not let anyone limit me...including myself.

At the time, I thought that was it. I had hit 160kg and it was 'lesson learned'. But that is quite dangerous really:

      a) to assume that you know everything.

      b) to think that you have hit a maximum.

      c) to believe that learning works that way.

Nevertheless, I did all three. I put myself back into a box – attached another limitation upon my life and kept myself way inside of my comfort zone. Even in the gym, I hadn't ventured much past 80kg in the years since 2020, meaning that my deadlifting weight was essentially at half of what it was. I told myself it was my injured knees that were the issue – but my knees carried the same injuries as they did in 2020. Then, I made excuses…that I didn't want to 'hurt myself' by lifting more – but I had a new trainer supporting me that was willing to help me with lifting practice. The last part was the worst part – I did not believe that I could do it.

So, I spent another three years in the gym. Frustrated at myself for what I perceived to be a lack of progress and being so hard on myself that I almost gave up.

Almost.

Then, a new challenge came along in 2023. It took me so far out of my comfort zone that I didn't recognise myself.

But that was the point.

It was a challenge that led to something new for me. Something I had always wanted but had not been able to fully grab hold of before…self-belief.

I had been waiting for self-belief to show up in my life. I didn't know how it was going to do it, but I imagined it would be in a loud, obvious way with signs pointing at it and a label that read "I believe in myself!" But it wasn't like that. It arrived quietly over time, made itself known and then allowed me to accept it.

My self-belief disguised itself in another deadlift. I was aiming for around 100-120kg this time. After all, I had not really lifted any heavier than 80kg in three years, and I was telling myself that I didn't want to hurt myself.

However, the challenge saw me lift more and more - going heavier and heavier each time…until suddenly, I was back at my old 'personal best' of deadlifting 160kg. But was it really my best, or was I capable of more? It turns out that the latter is true, and in late 2023, I surprised myself with a new deadlift – 180kg. **Grace moment.**

God has a way of humbling us and teaching us that the best plans are not ours at all, but his. The lesson for me, which is still being digested today, is to live in the moment.

There is no end point for growth…it is a continuing concept that happens throughout life – whether you are 'ready' for it, or not. Growth creeps up on you and takes you by surprise – moves you to a different place and then introduces you to its closest relative…change.

Growth and change are the two hardest things to do in life, but they are both necessary before life ends.

IX. Change

> *For you to become who you were meant to be,*
>
> *you must first let go of who you thought you were,*
>
> *say goodbye to who think you are,*
>
> *and redefine who you were hoping to be.*

The question is...how do you let go of who you have been? When you have been someone that you identify as strong, dependable, and reliable, how do you know who you will be if you let them go? When you have been a person that has survived 100% of your worst days, there can be a lot of fear surrounding even the idea of change. This is especially true if you're not sure whether the person you'll change into will be able to 'survive' like before.

Then there's self-doubt. What if I don't like who I become? What will I do if I'm unable to recognise myself? What if it doesn't work? What if I fail? Who will I be then?

I often have to remind myself that no-one is perfect – that it's part of the human condition to fail, that we all make mistakes, and everyone messes up. Even so, in all honesty…it feels different when it's you. We don't hesitate to encourage our friends, support family members and be kind to strangers. However, it feels different when we need to show compassion towards ourselves. This was especially difficult for me after experiencing mental ill health. Somehow, I had convinced myself that kindness was for other people and not for me – this was one of the hardest things that I had to start to change.

I have had my Bible from an early age. It was even with me when I had my episode of Psychosis, but I hadn't read it. I think this is because I was afraid of what I <u>thought</u> God was like. I thought I needed to be perfect for God to love me.

I didn't really understand how he cares or really appreciate that God only wants the best for us - and I mean <u>all</u> of us. For me, the closer I get to God, the more I am realising and learning about who he really is. His kindness, his forgiveness, his mercy, and his love.

There is so much that I want to say about what God has done and continues to do for me...and there really is no difference between you and me. There is nothing that I can do to make God love me more than he loves you. And there is also nothing that can be done to make him love any less. We are all his children, and he wants the best for each of us.

If there is one thing that you take from this book, please read the entire Bible at least once in your life.

The Bible has been indispensable for me in the process of change and healing. In times of trouble, worry, anxiety, fear, happiness, sadness, depression, anger, forgiveness, joy, grief, loss, and every storm of life: God is always there. I am always comforted and encouraged by Jeremiah 29:11.

It's a challenge for me too, but – let go, and let God. It was God that started a change in me...even though I am stubborn and say that I don't like change! I know that I would not be here – writing this book, recovered from Psychosis, or even alive, without him. He saved me.

Grace moment

X. Hope

My understanding of Psychosis today, is that it is a mental health illness that can include hallucinations, delusions of grandeur and paranoia. It can also affect your thinking and speech.

Some people have repeated episodes, whereas others may only have one in their entire lifetime. I hope and pray that I fall into the latter category. Psychosis taught me a lot about myself, but it is an experience that I would not want to repeat or go through again.

The thing is though – if I could go back in time and change it...I wouldn't.

What if God gave me Psychosis to save me from something that I was unaware of? What if it was God's way of 'waking me up'? What if this was a gentle and kind lesson to me about taking care of myself? What if it was a gift from God? What if it was designed to save my life and change me for the better?

Even though I didn't understand my Psychosis at the time, I have always said that "everything happens for a reason". There is also the fact that sometimes, God does not let you know things for your own protection. I feel a sense of peace in those parts of my episode that I do not remember – whatever I don't know, is God's way of keeping me safe.

Grace moment.

Ultimately, Psychosis brought me back to God. It helped me to discover and accept my authentic self. It is also an experience I can use to reach, inspire, and encourage others.

So, what would I say to anyone reading this right now?

Well...if you have experienced Psychosis yourself...I want you to know that you can recover.

You can get better.

It might take time, but it can happen. I know because I have been able to write this recovery story as a testimony of what God has done in my life.

If God can do it for me, he can do it for you too.

You are worth the time, the attention, the investment, the mistakes from which you will grow, the lessons from which you will change, the foundation upon which you will build, the space in which you can be yourself.

You are worth it.

Believe it. It is true.

Even if you have not had an episode yourself, you may know someone who has Psychosis presently, has had an episode in the past or may have one in the future. It could be that you are frightened about what this means for the person you know...or it may be that you are fighting feelings of guilt because you don't know what to do. This can be difficult, especially if you are wondering how best to support them. You might not be sure about how to broach the subject or be open to what they want to say.

The thing is...you might not comprehend why someone feels the way they do. You may not agree with their perceptions or know their experience and how it affects them. But what really helps, is having someone there to listen.

That is what really helped me. Having people around me, that were willing to listen to what I was going through.

They were willing to understand me.

Sometimes in life, you learn about other people being unwell. You may know someone that has an illness or suffers from a particular condition. Nevertheless, you don't seriously consider that it could happen to you.

Until it does.

Hindsight is 20/20. By that I mean, it is easier to see things looking back once you are <u>through</u> a situation, than it is when you are <u>in</u> the situation.

Whilst I do not want to ever have another episode of Psychosis...I consider that the one I did have, was as a **grace moment.** What I am learning, is that self-compassion, respect, and kindness are so important. In addition, gratitude and appreciation are key; be thankful for what you have and who you are. There is no one else like you, and only you can do what God created you for.

Mental ill health does not define you. It just means that you may have to look after yourself in a way that is different to others. You may have to introduce different boundaries to ensure that you have enough time for yourself and make time for self-care. Your working life will change, your relationships will change, and you may find that there are some things that are harder to do. However, your dreams are not lost, and life is far from over.

Whether you have experienced Psychosis yourself, know or support someone else who has...I write five messages here that I know to be true, that you can carry with you:

God Saves.

God Heals.

God has got you.

God loves you.

There is always Hope.

I'm still here, because of God's Grace.

…and that is how it ends from me…

Stay b.l.e.s.s.e.d.

Chelle.x

Printed in Dunstable, United Kingdom